all this light

Also by Ashish Bagrecha

Love, Hope and Magic

Dear Stranger, You Deserve to Be Loved

Dear Stranger, I Know How You Feel

all this love: Poems

POEMS

all this light

ASHISH BAGRECHA

HarperCollins *Publishers* India

First published in India by HarperCollins *Publishers* 2026
HarperCollins *Publishers* India, Cyber City,
Building 10-A, Gurugram, Haryana – 122002, India
www.harpercollins.co.in

2 4 6 8 10 9 7 5 3 1

P-ISBN: 978-93-6569-585-4
E-ISBN: 978-93-6569-729-2

Typeset in 12/14.2 Garamond at
HarperCollins *Publishers* India

Printed and bound at
Repro India Limited

MIX
Paper | Supporting responsible forestry
FSC® C047271

This book is produced from independently certified FSC® paper to ensure responsible forest management.

*

HarperCollins *Publishers*, Macken House, 39/40 Mayor Street
Upper, Dublin 1, D01 C9W8, Ireland

for everyone who ever hugged me.

maa used to tell me,
if you are given darkness,
you will also be gifted stars.
i never believed her,
until i wrote this book.

dear stranger (who isn't a stranger anymore),

when we first met through *all this love*, i shared my heart with you—raw, unfiltered, beating on every page. you held those vulnerable pieces of me with such grace, and for that, i am deeply grateful.

this book is different. this time, it's not just my heart i'm offering—it's my mind. the thoughts i've tried to quiet, the shadows that stretched too far. *all this light* is the other side of the story, where darkness meets the quiet persistence of light.

i'll be honest—writing this hurt. looking back at grief, loneliness, and pain was hard, but it was also healing. and by the end of this book, i hope you'll understand why.

some poems are heavy. take your time. let them sit with you, or let them go. there's no right way to navigate the darkness.

if *all this love* built a bridge between our hearts, this book connects our minds. it's a reminder that even in the darkest moments, we're not alone. someone else feels it too, and the universe is always watching over us.

so here i am again, offering not just poetry, but permission—permission to feel, to struggle, to heal, and to find your own light at your own pace.

with all this light (even in darkness),
ashish bagrecha

here i am, with another truth: every page here holds a piece of the storm, but also the calm that follows.

you might discover words that mirror your own struggles, verses that speak your unspoken thoughts. when you find those moments—fragments of truth that feel like they were pulled from your own mind—share them.

take a photo, share it online, tag me @ashish.bagrecha. it matters more than you know. in a world where mental health often hides in silence, your voice adds strength to these words. it tells someone else: 'your darkness is seen. your journey is understood'.

let me know which pieces of this collection echo your own story. it's why i write—to break the silence, to light the way for others walking similar paths.

a sound companion:

writing about mental health demanded its own soundtrack. here are the songs that witnessed every anxious word, every moment of healing and every glimmer of light i found while creating this book. they range from gentle piano pieces that soothed racing thoughts to powerful vocals that gave voice to what i couldn't say. consider them your musical guide through *all this light.*

scan to listen *(use your spotify app)* or
search 'all this light – ashish bagrecha' playlist.

happy healing and listening.

contents

prologue

i never asked for this—
this weight,
this burden
to be their salvation,
to save them from pain.

i grew up
in the dark corners of life,
but somehow,
the spark inside me
refused to die.

they look to me now,
their eyes full of questions,
full of expectations
i don't know if i can fulfill.

i found another way,
a life beyond the darkness,
but i learned long ago—
not everyone can be saved.

still, some part of me prays
i'm wrong.

so here i am,
a simple man,
a saviour of poetry,
a seeker of stars,
chasing *all this light*
to keep hope
alive.

all

can anyone fly
to the stars
to make sure
they haven't been replaced?

because their light
doesn't seem
to reach me
anymore.

i can't help
but envy the ocean,
for even its darkest depths,
the places no light can reach,
are called mysterious,
and not ugly.

nobody chooses sadness,
but we are human,
and sadness chooses us.

no one is free of it,
no matter how bright
their light may seem.

stop chasing light,
it's only a lighter shade
of your darkness.

no matter
how many times
you look into my eyes,
you will see nothing
but two flickering lights
slowly dimming,
starting to
burn out.

every night i stare at the stars,
waiting for some magic to happen,
hoping they would open up
and absorb me inside them.

sometimes i wonder
if hopes and dreams
are just pretty lies,
masked as beauty,
ripping you apart
from within,
when all the ugly things
in the world
couldn't tear you down.

einstein said
energy is neither
created nor destroyed,
it only transforms
from one form
to another.

little did he know,
so is pain.

sometimes
the heart gets broken
not by love
but by the idea of love.

why do i write?
is it to fill
the endless hole
left by the ones who came,
and never looked back?

is it to piece together
the wreckage they left,
or to speak the words
that my heart
needed them
to understand?

now i know
what is left
when a soul breaks apart?

just an empty shell
of someone
who no longer knows
how it feels
to exist,
to truly be.

stare too long at the sun,
and you go blind.
stare too long at the dark,
and you become it.

i wonder,
what does the universe
want from me?

shakespeare asked,
to be or not to be,
and called it the question.

but for me,
it's far simpler,
and far heavier:

to breathe or not to breathe?

some people
breathe through others,
as if their lungs
are filled with borrowed dreams,
living a life
that was never theirs.

some people
cling to fragments
of someone else's happiness,
desperately
craving a love
they can't find within,
yearning for a light
the world took away
from them.

to the ones i cared for,
i used to say,
'take my love
and trade your pain.'

little did i know
it would come true,
and i would have no idea
what to do then.

maybe my heart
was born too small
for all the love
it holds—

so it shares,
just to make
room to breathe.

i may not be able to stop you
when you decide to leave me,
but can i ask you to leave behind
a little smile, a little hug,
a little kiss, and a little love?

i will seize them in my heart
and use them as stars
in the lonely nights to come.

every time
i decide to leave you,
the entire universe
tells me to love you.

we're trapped in
a beautiful conspiracy.

you tell me
to forget it and move on,
but i don't understand—
how can i unfeel love
once i have felt it?

do you ever lose so much
that it feels like
everything is just waiting
to disappear?

like love,
a ticking time bomb,
every word
just another step
closer to the end
you can't stop
but can't bear to watch.

maybe everything happens
for a reason,
or maybe that's a lie
i tell myself
to forget you.

you made me homesick,
for the home i never had.

what is more painful:
to forget
or to remember?

once it was love
now it is a hole,
a gentle reminder
of what we lost.

to put it gently,
we call it a heartbreak.
in reality,
we feel destroyed.

i wish people
were more like shooting stars,
disappearing in a flash,
leaving only
the memory of beauty.

not like the sun—
unforgiving,
inescapable,
leaving us burnt
and burdened.

maybe the pain never stops
because i can't stop reading
hearts, eyes, and people.

all memories
leave a mark—
some are scratches,
some are scars,
and some
are the most beautiful tattoos.

i am not a poet,
i never was.

these words
coming out of me
are scared,
running for their lives,
desperately trying to escape
whatever is suffocating them
inside the heart
i carry with me.

how can i tell
if it's you i miss,
or just the way
you made me feel?

memories cling tight,
but nostalgia drifts,
in and out like tides
on a shore
only i seem to visit.

is it you
or the feelings we shared,
these little treasure chests
the sea sends back to me?

either way,
i will hold them close,
forever.

i would erase it all,
every word,
every line of poetry
i ever wrote for you,

if it meant
i could finally
free myself
from the hold
you refuse to release.

you and i,
mirrors of each other,
or maybe parallel lines
that never touch.

we are both lights,
too bright to belong together.
we were never made for each other—
we were made for the darkness.

our love healed me,
so fully,
so completely.

it only makes sense
that the same love
would shatter me,
break me apart
so wholly.

i loved you
with all of me—
my heart,
my soul,
my existence.

the broken pieces
that remain
are still yours.
come and take them,
or i swear
i'll throw them away.

my sadness,
why my soul feels scraped raw—
because everything i loved,
i loved recklessly.
and worse,
everything i loved,
i loved alone.

i try,
i swear i try,
to keep the shadows
from swallowing me whole.

but some nights,
the darkness is heavier
than the light
i carry inside.

and then it comes,
that heavy thought,
pressing itself into me:

maybe,
just maybe,
i was made
to be unlovable.

what would happen
if i strapped my heart
to a polygraph?

would it tell the truth
about the darkness inside,
or just lie to me
as it always does?

how strange it is,
this fear we carry—
the fear of losing someone
we long for most.

and yet,
it's that very fear
that keeps us
from ever having them at all.

all this light

i open my eyes
and realize
i am still alive
this morning.

only to be
reminded
that i will have to survive
one more night—
so cold,
dark,
and lonely.

chest pain so constant,
i have forgotten
how it feels
to breathe without hurting.

why do you stand there,
aching for the approval
of strangers,
when you can barely stomach
the weight of their presence?

oh, the irony
of wanting love
from those you cannot love.

is my air
different than others?
i can see
everyone living easily
while i can barely breathe.

how tragic that
our need to be held
is met by the fear of
being abandoned
one more time.

so all we can stutter
when someone asks,
'how are you?'
is
'i'm fine, i'm fine.'

we will say so much
about everything,
except what we
really want to say.

why is it
that we bottle it all up,
pretend we're whole
in front of strangers
who don't care,
who will never matter?

someone
lives inside my mind.

- confession

it hurts
to see what i see.

what hurts even more
is that no one else
sees it.

no one,
not a single soul,
will break your heart
like you do—

by overthinking
the pieces
that never needed
to fit.

dear diary,
my mind has become
too heavy to hold.

the world spins too quickly,
and my thoughts
chase it at a speed
i can't control.

society feels
like a foreign language,
its cruelty cutting deeper
than i can bear.

i don't know
if i can handle it anymore.

they say
hurt people
hurt people,

but they forget—
sometimes
the ones who hurt
and the ones who are hurting
are the same people.

- self destruction

i am worrying
about worrying—
living a life
of endless worry.

it is the mind,
always the mind,
that commits the crimes
we cannot see
against the body,
leaving it unsafe.

and the soul,
silent and weary,
stands witness
to it all.

the funny thing is
i always have to fight
even for air.

- anxiety

for better or worse,
life moves without
asking permission.

of course,
i am anxious.
as if it could be
any other way.

i used to thrive,
laugh and love,
wake with the morning breeze.

everything mattered,
yet nothing truly did.
i'd mess up and laugh about it,
my worries disappearing
with a cup of coffee.

now i survive,
smile and nod,
sleep as the sun rises,
wake up at night
feeling wrong.

nothing matters,
yet everything now does.
i mess up and shut down,
my worries
roar like storms.

i no longer strive.
my eyes search the ground.
please, world,
if you hear me,
just forget me—
let me go.

why is it
that darkness
always represents depression?

because no one
wants to face it,
no one wants
to see it.

because it's easier
to look away
than to truly see it,
to truly feel it.

no one stops to ask,
'why are you happy?'

but the moment
sadness shows itself,
the world leans in,
whispers,
'why are you depressed?'

as if the answer
would make it easier
to bear.
as if depression needs
to justify its existence.

i know,
deep down,
that i can do anything
i set my soul to.

so why,
in the stillness of it all,
don't i move?

depression is a struggle,
not just of the mind
or the heart,
but of the body too.

it steals the power
to make decisions,
leaving you lost
in a fog of indecision.

and somehow,
this uncertainty
cuts deeper
than the sadness itself.

the struggle is real,
leaving scars,
not just on you,
but on those
who love you.

the air i breathe
weighs heavy,
like bricks
piled in my chest,
a burden
i can't seem
to shake.

depression wraps itself
around me,
a spiral
pulling me deeper
into the dark.

i am calling for help,
but the echoes
barely make it
past my lips.

i wonder if anyone
can still hear me.

depression
can let you hope
to win the whole world
and become its king
for three straight days.

and on the fourth day,
it ties you
to the bed
with invisible shackles,
cunningly laughing at
how dumb
you are to think
you could escape it.

pulling you by the neck,
it whispers in your ear,
"forget the world—
you can't even win yourself."

you think you can defeat me?
never. i am my own downfall.

depression is a black cat,
its movements soundless,
its eyes watching
from the shadows.

it follows,
always,
and you never know
when it will pounce.

how funny that sometimes
we can't think anything,
yet our thoughts
become the end of us.

my depression
changed the colors
of the world,
painting it in muted blues
and endless greys.

and still,
somehow,
i've grown to love
the quiet beauty
of the shades
i now call home.

what if the world
was as frightening
as my mind whispers
it could be?

what if the monsters
i imagine
were never just
imagined at all?

then, i wonder,
would the world
know how to fight them?

headaches, heartbreaks,
cuts and scars.
aches in the body,
pains in the soul.

"doctor, give us something
to quiet it all,
to numb our brains."

everyone has a problem.
when did life become
a game
only pills can win?

they say
something's possessed me,
and i can't stop laughing.

why would a ghost
want to keep up with me
every minute of the day,
when a human hardly can?

one pill—
anxiety fades.
two pills—
panic attack stops.
three pills—
where is depression?
four pills—
where are you?
five pills—
where am i?
six pills—
who are you?
seven pills—
who am i?

sometimes i wonder
if my demons love me more
than my angels do.

maybe only the broken ones
know how to fix me up,
maybe only the empty ones
know how to make me feel whole.

beneath my bed
lies a box of pills,
each bottle labeled
with names
i can't even pronounce.

and yet,
with all these prescriptions,
not one
contains reassurance.
not one
fills the void
i carry.

this is going to work,
i tell myself.
paroxetine for fluoxetine,
hydroxyzine on top,
just pill after pill.
one of them
has to help.

but my head spins now,
i eat too much
or nothing at all.
i forget,
and i'm sorry
for all the forgetting.

to get better,
i must endure the illness,
the withdrawal,
the side effects.

funny how my cure
is also my illness.

the dark angel
visited again
and left
the marks on my back.

pills dull the pain,
but the storm lingers,
dark clouds waiting
to pour.

therapy, appointments,
the pills—they hold me up.
without them, i collapse
under the weight of myself.

my mind races,
but it's a losing race.
i'm fighting who i am,
and i'm losing.

they say death isn't the answer,
but tell me—what is?
i'm already dead inside,
and i hate what's left of me.

the demons don't go,
not really.
they only sleep
in the darkest corners
of the mind,
silent but never gone.

don't let them fool you—
they're waiting,
always waiting,
to rise again
and tear through
the soul
one more time.

nobody talks about
the side effects of trauma—
how it makes you
too forgiving,
too empathetic,
putting others first
just to avoid
the pain
you hope never returns.

tragedy
isn't even tragic anymore—
i'm just numb.

what hurt,
should hurt all the time.
and not make you numb
after a while.

it should not come
and go unannounced.

and if it's on the edge
of leaving, it should not turn back.

pain should not
play hide and seek
with you.

what hurt,
should hurt all the time.

and now
i'm not scared of pain,
i'm scared of not feeling pain.

i could drown
in burning water,
and still,
the coldness of my soul
would remain.

dear diary,
i wish i could say
i still feel,
but i don't,
not anymore.

sometimes i catch
a faint heartbeat
or the flutter
of a lonely butterfly,
but it's nothing
like the days
when i felt fully alive.

it's nothing
like the hope
that once carried me
through the dark.

'your eyes are the coldest
i have ever seen.'

- a note someone left on my table

i am afraid
of the moments
when the numbness fades,
when feeling rushes in
like a storm
i cannot escape.

terrified,
but alive.

my life splits itself
into two quiet extremes:
when i feel numb,
i crave something,
anything,
to remind me i'm here.

but on the days
when feeling comes,
i beg for the silence,
for the peace
of nothing at all.

one part of me
has surrendered,
the other part
has yet to begin.

this struggle is constant—
me battling me,

they trade victories,
each battle blurring the lines.
i'm weary, caught
between cheering for both,
each time.

it's a twisted game,
and the only player
is me.

my life is an act,
pretending,
always pretending.
and still,
it's never right,
never enough.

again and again,
i ask the world,
'why can't i be normal?'
but the world never answers.

i play every role,
every part i'm given,
but an actor
can't play two
in the same scene.

what do you want from me?
i don't understand.

i'm so tired.

i am tired.
not the mind kind,
not the eye kind.
it's the kind of tired
that lives in my bones,
in the blood
flowing through me.

this isn't a tired
from the world outside;
this is a tired
that starts inside,
a tired
that the world
will never be able to fix.

forgive me
if i need to pause,
to close my eyes,
to rest.
this kind of tired
is making me
tired of being tired.

i am not always this way.
but sometimes,
the world reminds me
how heavy
this tiredness can be.

the worst thing
about living here,
in the present,
is the memory of something
you once held in the past.

and the knowing,
deep in your chest,
that it's lost to the future,
never to be found again.

most things in life
don't matter—
they bring neither happiness
nor peace.

and so,
we keep searching
for something that does.
but does that something
even exist,
or is it just
a funny game
played by the universe
to keep us wanting?

on my tombstone,
don't etch the words:
died by accident
or disease.

let it speak the truth instead:
died in vain,
died from the quiet strain
of battles fought in silence.
he was killed
by his own brain,
his body an accomplice.
freedom,
if such a thing existed,
came only through his own hands.

write it clearly:
he died from the inside out—
can't you see?

it sends shivers through me,
how light outruns death.
how stars,
billions of years gone,
still defy time,
still burn across the cosmos
as if to say,
'you can't erase me.'

and it claws at my soul
to wonder
if the light i leave behind
will ever burn like that,
or if it will fade
the moment i'm gone.

what if,
just what if,
we are not the writers
of our stories?
a writer knows
what comes next,
but we are caught,
imprisoned by the pages
of the past and present.

some of us,
if we're honest,
barely live a story at all—
just characters
in someone else's plot,
or worse,
a tragedy
forgotten before it's finished.

if there is a god,
somewhere far away,
how does he choose?
how does he take
what we hold so tightly?
how does he decide
what is bad,
and why does it hurt so much?

if there is a god,
up there,
beyond the stars,
i hope he hears
my screams tonight.
i hope he sees
the hurt in my chest.

if there is a god,
how can he let this happen?
how can he be so distant,
so cruel,
and still call himself light?

tell me,
is your exhaustion born
from the endless tasks
you've taken on,
or is it the quiet burden
of the world's weight
pressing against your soul?

death, in its quiet way,
is the humblest of things.
it cares not for names
or titles,
it spares no one.
it is everything
that life is too afraid
to be.

to take your life
into your own trembling hands,
to believe escape
is the only way out,
might feel like freedom.
but know this:
to leave this world
is to bind the ones
who love you
to a prison
they never deserved.

i’m sorry
i’m sorry
i’m sorry
i’m sorry
i’m sorry
i’m sorry
i’m sorry
i’m sorry
i’m sorry
i’m sorry
i’m sorry
i’m sorry
i’m sorry
i’m sorry
i’m sorry
i’m sorry

- looking at the mirror

you're so afraid
of the monster you think
is waiting for you
in the distance,
you've ignored the storm
raging within,
and the quiet ache
in the hearts
of those who love you.

there's so much love here,
a lifetime of it,
but it's fading in the dark.
the thing you think you're fighting
is fighting me, too.

maybe,
just maybe,
the war i thought i fought
was never real.
maybe it was just me,
myself and my thoughts
all along.

they told me
my light would attract others,
little did i know
i'd have to burn for that.

now i know
home is not a housc,
or a town
or any place you live.
it is all the
light and dark
you carry with you
no matter where you go.

since its very beginning,
the universe
has never stayed
in the same place twice.
it's always shifting,
always moving,
always changing.

this is the cosmic truth—
nothing stays the same forever.
no being is final,
no feeling is final.

this

you think
no one can fix you,
but you don't know
some prayers are powerful
and some souls know magic.

how do i get back
all the light
i gave to the wrong people?

you handed me
all your broken pieces
but darling,
how do i fix you
when you don't believe in
love, hope and magic?

i understand—
if you can't trust healing,
at least trust
the possibility of healing.

you don't want peace
you want the chaos and storm
to bring you pain and destroy you.
you don't want to be found or loved
you want to stay lost and be left alone
but i won't let you.
every time you'll walk into darkness
i'll stand right next to you
and dare you
to destroy both of us.

of course, everything is crumbling.
your new life demands
the sacrifice of your old one,
a painful shedding
to embrace what's to come.

you are not a problem
that needs a solution.
you are not an error
that needs to be fixed.

it's easy to claim
life is meaningless
when you've never dared
to search for its truth,
never stood in the chaos,
seeking light
in the shadows.

i am sorry
for everything you went through.
i am proud of you
for still being here.
thank you.

sometimes it's okay
to tune out the world,
to walk alone
with your sadness.
there's no race
to healing.
there is no clock
ticking against you,
for to feel deeply,
to sit with the pain,
is what it means
to be human.

even if it was done to you,
it wasn't about you.

there's an art
to loving those
who are in pain,

a beauty in letting them
just be—
patiently waiting
for them to reveal
their scars,
their shadows,
their fragile dreams,
and finally
their light.

when life strips us
of what we thought we couldn't lose,
what remains
becomes more precious.

nobody should be allowed
to touch parts
of your home
and shatter them
on the floor
for you
to spend
the rest of your life
trying to pick them up.

parts even you didn't get
enough time to understand yet.

we are not our past selves,
we are merely a memory of our past versions.

stay in the sadness,
let it settle around you,
not as a burden,
but as a part of you.

stay,
until you're ready
to fold it away,
softly,
like an old coat
you no longer need.

your silence and
your disappearance
is not a story of weakness
but a tale of
survival.

follow me to the top of a mountain
or the middle of an ocean far, far away,
where no one can listen to us,
and let's cry our hearts out
until there is no pain left,
until there are no screams left.

let's empty our souls
till there is nothing else left,
but only light.

embracing
the inevitability of hurt
takes the power away
from the hurt
to hurt us.

you've a dark place in your heart
where all your dreams have died,
memories are chained,
love is buried,
and desires are murdered.
a haunted place,
even you don't want to visit it yourself.
but believe me,
i'm going to make that place my home
and rebuild it
with love, hope and magic.

yes i'm broken,
but i'm not for sale.

the more you
understand the world,
the harder it becomes
to hate it.

learning to be okay
with being alone
in a world so loud,
so full of noise
and temptation,
it's more than just
taking care of yourself.
it's an art,
a skill to master,
a quiet power
in a chaotic world.

if life is temporary,
how can anyone be permanent?
let them go.

this life
is a reminder,
a gentle promise
that there's another one
waiting for you.

do not fear the end.

the rest of your life
has just begun today.

when you're in a war,
there's only one way
to save yourself—
move forward.

i will dig a grave
in your soul
through my words
and bury my heart
inside it.
your soul can
never escape mine.

‘it’s ok,
you were just trying
to protect me.’
i forgave my mind
for all the anxiety it caused.

‘that’s always been the intent.
sorry, i didn’t know
the difference
between love and danger,’
anxiety replied.

if the demons
are sitting heavy
on your lungs,
stealing every breath,
i will press my lips
to yours,
and breathe life
back into you,
one breath at a time.

it’s okay
it’s okay
it’s okay
it’s okay
it’s okay
it’s okay
it’s okay
it’s okay
it’s okay
it’s okay
it’s okay
it’s okay
it’s okay
it’s okay
it’s okay
it’s okay
it’s okay
it’s okay
it’s okay

- looking at the mirror

sometimes,
we just need a hug—
for no reason at all.
to bury ourselves
in someone's arms
and somehow,
find ourselves there.

sometimes,
we just need the warmth
of skin against skin
to remind us
what light feels like.

how long would you hide in the dark
under the shadows of the moonlight,
waiting for the sun to rise?
you need to become the sun,
you need to try, you need to rise,
or risk your entire life
living in that darkness forever.

i will never tell you
to dismiss your sadness,
to compare your pain
to another's.
because sometimes,
being trapped
in your own mind
is the heaviest burden of all.

but even in that prison,
grace can slip through the cracks,
gentle and forgiving,
reminding you
that light will come.

you don't need
to make an effort to live.
you are life itself.
breathe.

what if
we all are fallen stars
and the moon is our guardian angel?

one day,
someone will look at you
and realize
your smile is the sunrise
they want to wake to
forever.
you will be the light
they choose
for a lifetime.

you don't need anyone's permission.
you are allowed
to hope.

stay alive
for the future you.
for the versions of yourself.
for the ones you haven't met yet.
for the ones waiting
to chase the light.

every mistake,
every misstep,
had to happen
to make you
who you are
right now.

trauma is a setup for transformation.

- life's biggest realisation

we all need saving,
and sometimes,
that means asking.
it means reaching
through the dark
with trembling hands,
asking for the light,
for someone to pull us
from the places
we can't escape alone.

loneliness is a universal feeling.
you are not alone.
i can assure you.

it may feel like it's not true,
but trust me,
you are your own story.
so fuck the doubts,
fuck the rules,
and write anything
that burns within you.

be a rebel,
a storyteller who refuses
to surrender
to the darkness.

i wrote all that we weren't,
but wished instead
for what could have been.

i hold no regrets,
no hate,
only gratitude—
even when it hurts.

if i'm to be blamed,
it's for sometimes
loving too much
and other times
loving too little.

we are small,
fragile things,
never as boundless
as the ocean.
yet, within each of us
is the power to ripple,
to touch the world
in ways
it will never forget.

in the darkest corners of despair,
hope dims,
and emptiness creeps in.
but even there,
you are not alone.

listen closely—
a heartbeat, faint yet steady,
urges you to rise,
to find the fragments of yourself,
to keep moving forward.

breathe deep.
let it fill you.
this is where love begins.
and when the time comes,
let the light
find its way to you.

the pain is over,
and so is the part of me
that cared for you.

i wish you could borrow
the eyes
of those who love you,
just for a moment.
maybe then,
you'd understand,
you'd believe
in the beauty you are,
and doubt
would never touch you again.

this time,
let people
find you.

there's no easy way
to face your darkness.
running won't save you—
it always finds you.
hiding won't help—
it will eat you alive.

you're stronger
and braver
than you know.
pain is just a piece
of your story,
not the whole picture.

lay it down,
bring it to the light.
universe knows your heart,
your needs,
your worth.

to universe,
you are always enough.

pain lies,
depression lies,
anxiety lies,
fear lies,
loneliness lies,
hopelessness lies,
self-doubt lies,
silence lies,
mind lies,
the night lies,
and even the darkness lies.

none of them
stay forever
no matter what
they say.

maybe we never completely heal,
maybe we just heal enough.
enough to feel again.
enough to love again.
enough to live again.

every night,
i fight for my life.
and every morning,
i wake proud,
knowing i've succeeded
at something.
grace is there,
in every breath i take,
a quiet reminder
that i am stronger
than the darkness.

in the quiet hours of dawn,
light lifts me higher,
whispering,
'you've done enough.'

they trust the universe
and its flow.
but what does it mean
to follow it?

to speak your desires
to the cosmos,
to trust
that the people,
the struggles,
the moments—
are all part of the plan.

don't question it.
don't give up.
trust the flow is real,
and go with it.
willingly.
for even in the darkest times,
the universe leads you
toward the light.

always wait for the stars.
always.

this life was given to you
by someone.
so tell me—
what will you do about it?
what will your answer be
when asked
how you lived it?

and will you say,
you lived it with grace?

freedom is already inside you,
not something to chase,
but something to remember.

the past taught you to survive,
but this moment teaches you to live.

the future is waiting,
kind and clear,
a new timeline
aligned with your soul.

no scripts,
no algorithms,
no interference.
just you,
finally free to be.

i am not scared now,
the pain has ended,
i am an ocean of memories,
i have nothing to hide,
my words have defeated silence,
i have nothing to lose,
i am chaos in its most beautiful form,
i am the light of a darkened soul.

- the awakening

light

they tell me
that no light can enter
or come out of
the blackhole
inside you,
but they don't know
the magic of poetry.

there is no darkness in you,
there is so much light
that even the darkness
is attracted towards you.

promise me
you'll stay alive
so that one day
when i'm in your city
we can go for a coffee,
talk about the stars,
and share our stories
of love and hope.

promise me
you won't give up
so that the universe
gives us a future
we deserve.

if the sun doesn't reach you
and you've given up
on the stars and moon,
i'll break myself
into a million pieces
and sprinkle them
across the sky,
to send you light
and save you
from your depth of darkness.

if all you want is only darkness,
then i can rip out all the stars in the sky,
but i'm sorry
my heart cannot stop glowing for you.
you can have a starless sky
and a moonless night,
but i'm sorry
my soul will always send you light.

the heart breaks,
and at last,
it sees
all the light
it carried
all this time.

not today
not today
not today
not today
not today
not today
not today
not today
not today
not today
not today
not today
not today
not today
not today
not today

- everyday warning to death

in the deep black sky
even though a million miles apart,
the sun still finds a way
to bring light to the moon,
and you expect me
to leave you in this darkness.

you are made of stardust,
every inch of your body
was once a part of the galaxy.
when you hate yourself,
you hate the universe.

to find the light,
i tell myself,
is to find hope.

but every night,
my mind whispers burdens
i cannot bury.
the voices drag me
into the dark,
stab at my heart,
and leave me
broken, gasping.

sometimes,
you become the dark
just to survive.
you shatter what controls you,
cling to what's left of yourself,
and swear
to never let go.

to find the light,
you let go,
you hope.

the entire universe is mine,
and yet i'm lost
in search of something
to call my home.
how foolish of me.

you turned my hollow bones
into something whole,
a loving home built
on the courage
it takes to endure.
you taught me that resilience
isn't about never breaking—
it's about rebuilding,
over and over,
and that rising,
again and again,
is the bravest thing
i'll ever do.

you don't need anyone to shine,
you are a sun, not a moon.

you will die this way,
trying to hold the universe
on your back,
as if the stars would shatter
without you.

the chaos you cling to
is ripping through you,
tearing your soul apart,
turning light into void.

let it go.
set it on fire,
let the ashes scatter
and smile.

you are not the savior
of the stars.
you were never meant
to carry their weight.

drop it.
let the universe
carry itself.
trust me,
the stars will not fall,
but you—
you will finally rise.

you are
the chaos of the cosmos,
light spilling from cracks
in your soul.

if they can't handle
the way you burn,
let them close their eyes,
stars don't apologize
for their fire.

don't you know
you are loved?
not just by life,
but by the stars themselves—
burning brighter
just for you.

don't you see
your past is dust,
scattered in the cosmos?
you are galaxies unbound,
a force,
brilliant and untouchable.

don't you feel
the fire inside you?
a raging light
the darkness can't extinguish.
you are more—
more than fear,
more than doubt,
you are everything
the universe fights to keep alive.

i have stars inked all over my body
in the form of scars,
and every time you will touch me,
they will emit light.

into the darkness,
drag your fire.
when hope is crushed
and shadows choke,
let your spirit rage,
refuse to be broke.

through storms that tear,
through pain that screams,
be the light
that burns through dreams.

let the dark know
it cannot win.
carry your fire—
again, and again.

the moon reminds me of you,
how beautifully you both try
to fight the darkness.

i know the stars died in you
and that's how you became
the home of darkness.
but i want you to go
into the unknown
and find a new home.
please remember
you're an explorer
of love, hope and magic.

like the moon,
we all go through phases
just to feel whole again.

death will come to you
the very moment when you're of no use,
when you've nothing more to give,
when no one needs you.

you being alive is the reminder
that somewhere someone out there
is searching for you,
that someone still needs you,
that you've so much more to give.

the heart mends
and at last,
it learns
why it broke
in the first place.

all this light

i feel my heart beating,
and for the first time,
i'm not hiding.
i'm fighting,
winning,
smiling,
alive again.

i feel the touch
of the earth,
the moon,
the stars.
i have my soul,
and now i know
it's worth it to fight,
worth every night.

even when the darkness calls,
there's light
waiting to find me.
and though i will fall,
i won't stay down,
because inside me,
there's a fire
that refuses to fade.

what if we are fallen stars
who've forgotten their origin,
and are looking at the sky
trying to remember
what home felt like.

i've spent my life
chasing stars,
not to claim them
or call them mine,
but to feel the burn of hope
on my hands,
reminding me
i am alive.

the sky,
that endless expanse,
was never meant
to be touched—
only to be reached for,
even when it hangs
just out of reach,
teasing the dreamers
who dare to try.

maybe the reason
why you are feeling restless is
because the universe is trying
to tell you something
and the stars are trying
to talk to you.

- listen to them

dreams whisper softly,
stars fall like tears.
hearts beat wildly,
but love conquers fears.
hope grows,
time heals,
and forever,
light is ours.

only two things last forever:
death
and true love.

everything else—
sorrow, anger, pain,
jobs, friendships, possessions—
is temporary,
fading with time.

take comfort in this:
you are not bound
by what feels endless now,
only by death,
and love,
the two infinities
that define us.

the universe is fighting to keep you alive.

- daily reminder

i hope you win
all the wars,
you fight alone,
the ones
you tell no one about.
may the darkness within you
one day
give way to all this light
you've always deserved.

i think i'm ready now,
ready to know what it feels like
to live my dreams.

what sacrifices will i make,
what joys will find me,
and what sorrows?
will the coffee taste richer,
the stars burn brighter,
or will they dim
under the weight of it all?

life, it seems,
has a soft spot
for the bold,
because too many of us
wait too long
to chase what we desire.

but not me.
not anymore.
i'm ready.

all this light

i love the stars
because their light takes millions of years
to reach me.
i'm staring into the past
every time i look up,
wondering if the star
is even still there.

it's the uncertainty that gets me—
it makes me feel things
i used to bury deep.

if a star can shine long after it dies,
then maybe,
when i'm gone,
a piece of me will linger too,
a light
still reaching someone's eyes.

the stars make death
feel less terrifying,
less like an end.

they never understood
how i burned through
a hundred lives,
how i died ninety-nine times
just to crawl back to the surface.

they lived one life,
wrapped in fear,
while i became
every version of myself,
again and again.

they didn't see
that it wasn't bravery—
it was survival,
a raw, relentless need
to keep moving,
to keep burning,
even when the darkness
was all i knew.

i am proof
that even after ninety-nine deaths,
you can still rise
to live your hundredth life
and make it worth it.

the world has disappointed you,
the universe will not.
trust me on that.

we fear the dark,
but how can we fear
what we don't allow ourselves
to feel?
it doesn't disappear
when denied—
it waits,
it absorbs,
it becomes part of us.

darkness isn't the enemy.
it's part of you,
just like the light.
the place where
truth lives.

that sometimes,
the light you seek
is hidden
in the darkest part of you.

you must embrace
all of you.

the world can cause me
all the pain it wants.
it can take away
every person i love.
it can break
every bone in my body,
create chaos in my mind.

but it can't destroy my love,
it can't steal my hope,
and it can't kill my magic.

i wasn't a poet then.
because i looked at my skin
and saw only paper,
cutting it open
as if it meant nothing.

i wasn't an artist then,
because i painted over scars
that i didn't want to see.

but now,
i hold both titles,
poet and artist,
not by their rules,
but by the rhythm
of my own heart.

i am human,
a galaxy of words and stars,
a cosmic collision of poetry.
i am both calm and chaos,
with a light
that reaches the infinite.

all this light

remember,
your past may be damaged,
but that doesn't mean
your future has to be.
even in the darkest chapters,
all this light
waits
to rewrite the ending.

i may've
struggled all my life
with pain, heart-break
and darkness,
but from now on,
i shall never forget
that i'm made of
love, hope and magic.
that i'm the home to
all this light.

all this light

even though we feel
like we live our lives alone,
through every heartbreak,
every failure,
every loss,
every tear we've shed,
and every time we gave up,
someone was always there,
watching.

only if we looked up
from our self-centered lives,
we'd see the stars,
always there,
living alongside us,
never leaving.

they've been shining,
smiling all this time,
because they already knew
what we didn't—
that one day,
we'd discover the magic
within ourselves.

one day,
we'd look up at them
and smile right back.

only if we had the eyes
to look through each other
we'd understand
that inside our fractured hearts
we all carry
an exceptional magic
to heal each other.

here i am,
small and infinite,
learning to breathe
in the vastness of a universe
that feels both cruel
and kind.

i once knew nothing,
believed nothing.
but now,
these emotions i hold,
these storms inside me,
are not meaningless.

they are the stars imploding,
releasing light,
reminding me
that even destruction
has purpose.

and somehow,
in the debris of it all,
i am healing.
i am becoming alive.

i am just me,
a poet fumbling
through a world
too beautiful for my words.
i don't have the elegance
of perfect lines
or the rhythm
they write books about,
but i have my stories,
and they are mine
to keep.
no one can take
what lives in me.

the universe has already written
all the stories
you're going to read, tell and live.
it has already decided
all the people
you're going to meet, love and lose.
all we got to do is
trust the universe and its flow,
because it already knows
all the places
you're going to
find happiness, dreams and hope.

maybe the universe
didn't send you
to connect the dots
or solve life's mysteries.

maybe you're here
to share the fire
burning within you
with the souls
lost in darkness.

i live my life
through you.
it's incredible,
like living two lives at once.
i walk alone,
but our hearts beat as one.
i sleep alone,
but we dream the same dream.
through you and me,
i am in two places at once—
until we reunite
and become each other's light.

if life was only a day,
what would we do with it?
would we dream
without time
to bring those dreams to life?
would we fight,
without time to heal?

love might barely arrive,
pain might never linger.
in the endless expanse
of infinite time,
perhaps our life
is nothing more
than a fleeting day.

maybe that's all we are—
a single day
in infinite time.

but even one day
can be enough.
let it be a day
we're proud of,
a day that mattered—
well lived,
well felt.

love is what brings
our dark souls together.
love is the light between us.

in the end,
i am certain,
we all are nothing
but
all this light.

neither created
nor destroyed
only transformed
from one form
to another.

epilogue

i carried the weight,
their questions, their pain,
a burden i never asked for
but bore anyway.

i stumbled in the dark,
my spark flickering,
fighting against shadows
that whispered, "you can't."

but i found something
in the emptiness,
something that wasn't meant
to save them—
but to save me.

not every star burns forever,
not every soul can be saved.
i learned that,
and still,
i chased the light.

and now,
as the final words fall from my pen,
i see it—
the stars i sought
weren't in the sky,
but within me all along…

…all this light,
it was mine to carry,
mine to share.
not as a savior,
but as a simple man,
still searching,
still healing,
still alive.

this is not the end.
this is the moment
i realize
i was never chasing the light.
i was becoming *all this light.*

dear stranger,

this book was born from the edges of life—from foggy days, depressing nights, anxiety attacks, and conversations with different therapists.

to you, who held these heavy words—thank you. these poems are fragments of my mind's darkest corners, now shared with yours. if they helped you feel less alone, if they gave words to your own struggles, then these pages have served their purpose. in a world that demands we mask our pain, i hope this book reminds you it's okay to be vulnerable and share how you really feel inside out.

to those who walked with me through the shadows—you gave me courage to write these truths. thank you for seeing me, even when i couldn't see myself.

to my family and friends—you witnessed my battles, my breakdowns, my slow crawl toward light. you sat with me in silence when words failed. these pages exist because you never let me fade away.

carry these words with you. let them remind you that your struggles are valid, your journey matters, and that light always finds a way back, even through the smallest cracks.

with all this light,
ashish bagrecha

in these times
of filtered feeds
and masked minds,
talking about darkness
feels forbidden.

so believe me
when i say,
this raw truth
is getting harder to find.

share these words
with those who struggle.
let them know
they're not alone.

About the Author

Ashish Bagrecha is a bestselling author and one of the most loved Instagram poets in India. His books *Dear Stranger, I Know How You Feel and Love, Hope and Magic* have sold lakhs of copies. Ashish is also a popular audio creator, and you can listen to his podcasts and shows on Audible and Spotify. For more information on his books, tours, podcasts and projects please visit www.ashishbagrecha.com or @ashish.bagrecha on Instagram.

Bestselling titles by Ashish Bagrecha

all this poetry series

all this love
all this light
all this life

find out all about the books, tours, podcasts and projects
at www.ashishbagrecha.com

HarperCollins *Publishers* India

At HarperCollins India, we believe in telling the best stories and finding the widest readership for our books in every format possible. We started publishing in 1992; a great deal has changed since then, but what has remained constant is the passion with which our authors write their books, the love with which readers receive them, and the sheer joy and excitement that we as publishers feel in being a part of the publishing process.

Over the years, we've had the pleasure of publishing some of the finest writing from the subcontinent and around the world, including several award-winning titles and some of the biggest bestsellers in India's publishing history. But nothing has meant more to us than the fact that millions of people have read the books we published, and that somewhere, a book of ours might have made a difference.

As we look to the future, we go back to that one word—a word which has been a driving force for us all these years.

Read.

Harper Collins · Harper Sport · HARPER FICTION · HARPER NON-FICTION · हार्पर हिन्दी

HARPER LEARNING · HARPER VANTAGE · HCCB HARPERCOLLINS CHILDREN'S BOOKS · 4th · HARPER PERENNIAL

HARPER DESIGN · BOOKTOPUS · HARPER BUSINESS